Love, God, Cats and Other Mysteries.

Ivan Podwys

BookLeaf Publishing

India | USA | UK

Presentation by *BookLeaf Publishing*

Web: www.bookleafpub.com

E-mail: info@bookleafpub.com

ISBN: 9789357214742

First edition 2022

To my Family, Friends, and Educators,
Thank you.

Four Favorite Animals

I like to watch cats play.
Feline furiosity, chasing flys fantastically.
The hallway superhighway, Down, Up, Down.
Then Sleep, 14 hours, anywhere Sleep.
Sometimes I wish I was a cat.

I'd watch a mouse fly past for dinner.
Running, nimbly, sprightly, catching prey.
The den, all mine, free as my will can stand.
With no bills to pay and no jobs to keep, I'd
sleep.
But I wouldn't learn why the sky is blue.

I like to watch ferrets play.
Mustelidae frivolity, flipping fantastically,
The War Dance, while hissing and clicking.
Then Sleep, 18 hours, anywhere Sleep.
Sometimes I wish I was a ferret.

Going anywhere, no city line or country divide.
I'd watch the moon and hunt all night.
With no house to clean and no chores to keep,
I'd sleep.
Jumping, twisting, dancing, catching prey.
But I wouldn't learn to value any art.

I like to watch dogs play.
Canine fabulously focusing fantastically,
The ball, OH WAIT SQUIRREL.
Then Sleep, 13 hours, anywhere Sleep.
Sometimes I wish I was a dog.

Stalking, waiting, chasing, catching prey.
With no political plays and no favors to keep, I'd
sleep.
I'd watch the moon and howl when I please.
Never alone, I'd always have my pack.
But I wouldn't learn to read or write.

I like to watch foxes play.
Vulpine fancy, fearless, fantastically
Felicitous, Raspy barking sweetly.
Then Sleep, 10 hours, anywhere Sleep.
Sometimes I wish I was a fox.

With no games to play and no worries to keep,
I'd sleep.
My beautiful coat would be second to none.
Prancing, digging, marking, catching prey.
I'd watch the sunset and enjoy my kin.
But I wouldn't learn to value my heart.

Sometimes it's better to be human.

Valley of Dreams

Within my mind is a valley of dreams, it sits in
betwixt mountains high.
Standing by my vivid memories and rapid
swirling emotions
 I stare outward. This place, well it seems like
magic. I'm spinning yet, standing,
Within an Inward blanketed embrace of words
thriving in devotions.
Lifted off my slatestones, on great wings I'm
standing betwixt seeing ear and silent eye.

I look out over Limitless landscapes, infinite
towering constructions.
Landing on a barren precipice of organized
crystals I see it all.
Constructs of transparent creatures fly past and
return. On landing
I Inquire, "transparent wonders, words of
wandering, where am I," I call?
In rhythmic oscillations they answer "Welcome
to times landing, in dreams matter organizing."

Here all creation happens and herein lay the
foundations of the soul.

Branding the illusion of the impossible possible
and all things Probable.
Everything happening intrinsically, herein all are
stamped in your branding.
All that you create becomes foundations for real
world solvables
Applications for branding the work of real
experiences made whole.

I look out, psychic hands, invisible to
understanding, shaping lucid dreamscapes,
Demanding my attention, cerulean futures seek
unimagined swirling seminations.
Here all creations emanate, spinning forth into
existence, Demanding
I see through hadean filters, thriving beginnings,
emanating emancipations.
Within the valley of dreams, a demanding
confluence of complex landscapes are set free.
And Head lifted from slatestone pillows I create
my true reality.

Guilty Anger

The monster lies within, it escapes not easily. I
wish it weren't so.
Why won't it leave the demon inside fighting
Thought its way to the surface?
What makes life real, the fool's imagination of
reality?
Lie inside the conscience-mending mind
They lay splayed open on the floor, displaying
all that is within.
The monster seeks them. He wants to let the real
dissolve imagination
To make the demon real. It attacks the mind.
There is no escape from the grasp.
One will fight back or succumb, succumb to
death.
No death of body, but sanity gone far below the
surface of the life within.
Where does the selfish lie make known real the
empty death of dangerous demon minds?
When will I control it? Can I gain the control
that I need for that sanity I seek?
The balance never-ending, ending off-key.
When will sanity rain on the demon and the
darkness

Can it be done, till death or only in the
hereafter?
When does it end the pull of darkness,
The hunger? To crave for it, that thing that
cannot be seeked.
Can it be that it is a permanent state of being to
suffer for that forbidden taste of knowledge?
Does knowledge meet its day at the end of days?
The limits must be found. Exorcize the free,
release the bound
Another day to fight again. More truth to see and
see we do.
When it leaves, The demon of violence in envy
He calls. Kill and destroy the world, no reality
exists
The self only is the concern. So unwise and of
one mind
He can be defeated, the monster of guilt
dispelled by his own greed.
No longer a prisoner again but when will it
return, the cycle never stops till the end in death.
The struggle is real. Let it ride, pit the demon
and monster to the life of defeat, not today alone
But for a time, there is peace of mind.

Of Book Dreams and Nightmares

The week was like a dream.

The days felt endless and deep.

The stacks of paper looming and

The empty boxes with menace staring.

The bags once full of groceries empty,

Now full of idle writings screaming.

Thin Hungry plastic swelling, classics and

Speculatives equally eaten, engorged.

Carried on heavy shoulders, a hulk

Of dead trees headed to new homes.

Ten they flew and yet remained dozens

more to be broken open to hearing eyes.

How is it that with ten bags gone

so many remain unopened? Perhaps

one day they will all be seen, the mountains left

to scale, the reading of words yet left unopened.

We Existed

A painting, a flat representation of things past,
Colorful in textured plastic tones of rubberized
crust,
Measured and poured and spread to cover
The wonder of loss, seemingly forgotten in
existence.

A painting of pregnant memories, hidden and
revealed
By pictures of the forgotten seeking a
remembrance.
You call me from somewhere else as if time
herself
Could look out from the crust of eternity to catch
my gaze.

Time, a mistress of shifting sands, a loyal desert
of history,
In her intergalactic glass frame, pulling me
through painted matte,
Chemical batched prisons forming rubber
frames, holding visual souls
Of the condemned, kept frozen in a
representation of the millions.

Thin bodies and bruised faces sink below the
globular mass of buried earth,
The rainbows of plastic temporal earth flowing
over you all.
Your features painted over by present pressing
persistent conflicts.
Yet you stand in darkened sunset covered in pale
washes,
Tinted by opinions politically possessed and
devoid of consciousness.

Your eyes watch me, taking in my reactions, and
guiding my visual direction.
Speaking from an orange-tinted camp of fear,
repressed by a busy world.
Your purple processed possessions, stolen for
great warehouses of greed.
The enterprising entrance of exterminators in
cold winter open to view.
Brick block buildings of heroic monsters
claiming their gated victims.

I see you

Wanting to claw through this painted canvas I
unfasten the bounds of reality and time.
And in my mind, I reach in and save those guilty
of no wrong, cursed for who they are.

Souls different in beliefs or personal expression,
Hated all, for ever existing.

But time does not her chapters open or her
travelers set free.
So I study Your faces, Your voices, Your
mournful and defiant captured expressions.
Hopping wherever you are now, you never see
us repeating again such cruelty.

Elegy for Ukraine

When war comes calling no one really wins.
The dead cannot celebrate hollow victories.
The red loss of blood stains the victor.
Time leads only forward, strained weeping
When warriors, civilians must make.

Heroes, of everyday life stand forth fighting.
Valiantly defending their home country.
Like lions they resist the conqueror
Protecting their freedom and their families.
While the world fights with words and
Promises for protection that never comes.

With hope, they stand to defend, small
Victories costing greatly. The powers
Whisper and wail threatening's and
With sanctions damage the enemy of the people.
At least they are taking a side, and
In the end, this may make all the difference.

Then You Were Angry

I watched you both, standing stern in decadent
defiance,
Ears bleeding, the silent sentient scratching of
discordant fears
Minds covered in optimistic storm clouds gone
snow drift.
Where was the ancient integrity, the
once-blossomed beauty?
Whom, when wind angered quickly, furry you
became?

To the second participant, I say much the same
again.
The fire of past relationships, memories still
stinging the rainbows,
Discolored in saturated hues of now darkened
loves.
When did fire & ice become the angry tiger
slaying its protesting prey?
Disappearingly silent, stoking the flame, you
have become the tiger.

Both minds closed, equally appearing murderess
in eyes of open greys disarrayed.

The swamp of self-discoveries, past mistakes
subconsciously borne,
Eating the flesh of time like prolific fleas biting
and barking profanities.
Where did I go amiss your superbly supporting
faces?
Failed I did, to equate your separating distances?

At the marrying division of wife and mother,
awkward with fear, change is hard.
The abusive sun melted the exterior renderings
of your embracing potentials
Fists became stones and stones throwing
boulders of discontent remembrances.
Redheads, napalm passions, sparking each
surface kindling, bleed vehemently.
Why is it separation couldn't heal electric
plasma fissures of past lives?

Horrid melodies replacing honey-enclosed
ballads when nearby entangled.
Moon dancer, separating each performance from
reality in traumatic waves of red tides.
Dissolving cement barricades of synaptic logic
with surgical precision.
Cold-hot emotions let willingly free, ripping
silk-silicone love, and why?
Pasts so distantly close that scarred memories,
presently active, burn through.

0 HELLO 1

It stares at me, waiting, patiently waiting for me
Soon to be alive, awake, running, and breathing
It calls and I answer, I walk to it, slowly stalking
My great hand greets it, gripping the emerald
light
Awakening the growling Beast and dust beneath

I imagine myself a particle, standing and staring
At towering energy silos in gray, brown, and
blue
Observing a green grass city with copper roads,
Black office blocks on flat skyscraper walls, and
Its whirlpools of spinning air and cooling tubes

I know its internal playground of spinning
hamsters
Its slides and tunnels of lightning packages
I know its freeways its gates and its crosswalks
Its dry savannah of windy open plains and
I know its warehouses, power plants, and
factories

It sits there a cold cubic block of metal and
plastic

still as a frozen desert rock to the outward
human eye
Intelligence feigned by Inner wisping whispers
Precious, it appears in a coat of silver and black
One emerald upon it, bright, flashes back at me.

Hello Computer

Hello User

I sit here daily, waiting, patiently waiting for you
soon awakened, quiet, copper strings, onward
moving
I call back, wind-whispered, walking the
roadway
Upward I meet it, liquid rainbow ocean
Coordinating crystalline communication
I imagine myself made of flesh, staring back
At towering mind with fur in gray, brown, and
red
Observing a geeky green gamer with copper
rings,
Black office chair and rice paper balls, and
The research pools of winning codes and
computing tools

I know your eccentric playground of endless
searches
Your twenty browser tabs and Amazon packages

I know your neurology, phonology, and
iconology
Your many programs of open-world psychology
I know your moods, diet plans, and fantasies

You sit there an organic skinned version of me
Still as a desert hawk watching my copper
memory travel
Intelligence engaging my outspoken silence
Precious, with senses, reacting in suits of plastic
wrap
Two glittered eyes upon me, lightning blinking,
responding.

01001000 01100101 01101100 01101100
01101111 00100001

Aren't We All a Little…

Certain I was in all my
arrogance fully colorblind and
so tolerant of all yet nothing in
my ignorance did I know
the difference. So learn I did yet slow
I bid my metal mental mantle to stimulate
simple simulation.
Resistant to hearing truth in myself, the
double-dipped distressful dissidence
of diversity broken. Love for all I held in
wooden shack, wolf blown down I can't turn
back. Faced by my mirror lacking, the colors of
belief mudded by revelating. Insularity facts
now glide with vision fleeting, finding
purchase, on bias mountain seaside, I see what I
couldn't. In the depths of cultural programmatic
performances, none are free from internal
inadequate insecurities of otherly obscurity.
Open discourses bloody bewilderment
besieging, now principally piercing hiding hefty
heart. Serious stoic self
cautiously considering catalogs of newly
acquired references, personal recollections of
diverse experiences.

Emotions in murky overwhelming
realizations of anvil weighted doubt, in
understanding, I come forward
                with desire, to understand
unknown undervalued utterances of centuries.
Colorblind no longer I
                seek another anchored authority.
Whitewashed walls withering away revealing
vulnerable core
                melting and reshaping. Teach
me while I am here,   tell me the tattered
titular truth
                                of
self-experience.
Expand my awakened
    mind & yearning
            heart.

How to Escape a Running Train With a Paper Airplane

How do escape a running train when it runs
inside your head and it runs randomly through
your mind?

When the storms of life gather and distract the
tracks to hither, thither, and yon.

If you can't find an option try this novel solution,
put yourself on a plane on that train.

Crazy you say? Well try it someday and see just
how far it will take you.

You trick it you see with a puzzler like these,
that follows a silly suggestion.

Why can't I fly a Paper Airplane coated in tinfoil
to the moon on a Thursday afternoon when the
sky is golden blue and make it back in time for
dinner?

And if doesn't do, try this one I do.

If my plane is a turkey how far will it go?

Addictive Truth

Reality is disconnected in
Distant discordant dissident color;
Wake, awake, up, escape this hell in thee.
Run from hiding, don't give in, don't yet flee,
Why let em win? Give up the fight? Nay, nay!
I will fight, I will proceed the fight, fae
Darkness, fae sleep, awake to live, live not die.
My fight is right, to fight, escape the night,
Do not now hide from fear in open sight.

Let it come, but only be now prepared
To never invite and never yet dare.
No sin, I can win then will I escape
From lust, greed, hate, and depression's great
weights.
My pulse? is it strong? my vitals lay weak,
Long dying, rebuilding, strengthened but meek.
The edge is in front, but I will not jump
Off ledge, in a stunt, the charges up trumped.
Don't let the mind race above the soul's light.

Keep control of the fight for truth for life
Keep in check, inside, all I find not right.
I will not fade in the dark of my mind,
Fight the heart's war off the life support line.

Keep fighting strong let not fear thus abide
Do not hide from truth let truth now decide
Am I now faded, forced-betrayed from right,
My pulse playacted by another's sight
Heart's controls not my own, soul loud affright.

The end not in sight I fight back fight fight.
Gravity pulls my soul to dark or light
Bright like a nebulous hourglass pulsar
Let the help enter in and fly, pull me far
Away, strong and alive. Free of the blood
Addictive knife that stabs the soul in floods
Of wasted hours' time. Rescue now away
Bray fire in the mind, molten flowing brae
Nowhere to run to, to hide out of sight.

Don't pull the plug on life I'm not done yet.
Remove the knives from my side, let eyes see
Situation's truth, universal depth

Of possessed decay. Observe now the breadth,
The height, the reach of the addictive wave.
Prepare for war! GET UP. Prepare for war!
I must forget but first forgive my mind,
Knives digging twisted mental imagery
Prepare for war! GET UP. Prepare for war!

The pressure stinging, I pull them free and
Silence the doubt, the daggers of the mind.

The memory that identifies me
All that my mind has thus betrayed to me
They will no longer define my true self.
Misunderstood my heart bursts free it's shelf.
The pieces down aground pick up the wreck
Searching something better all hands on deck
Put em together not give em away.

I will repair the lost connections of
Family 'n Friends. Use powerful cord
To wrap the healing wounds, with patient time
Spent, til the fire of faith in self, full-time
Given, re-fuses us together, like
Molten glass refined. The night is starlike
Yet not far off the sun will rise again.
Let day burn the night. Let recovery
Begin. I'll survive, I will thrive, Today.

Today, I will survive!

4's 5's and 20 to live

I

A Living hourglass of twisted fate, er' filling &
draining by choices made
Distant realities disconnected, discordant
dissident truths malaligned
Emotions in fluidic drifting flight, living but not
alive, awakening
Past chains by persistent purpose broken, live
fae past bespoken foreboding
Wake, awake, up, escape this hell within, eyes
wide awake, forward momentum
make.

II

Broken but not forgotten memories, imperative
resolute resonance
An incongruous impersonation, of this
phantasmagoric masquerade
In safe surreptitious simulacra, a solipsistic
singularity
Impertinent esoteric id, fuel for dreamer's fire
forming features
Informative contextual contents, programmatic
of prospective designs.

III

Escaping Hypnos' infinite vision, rainbows of
imagination made real
Silence the doubting daggers of the mind,
fathomed darker self-mirrored reflection
A ravenous vespertine manticore, running on to
disencumbered freedom
The dreamer living in auspicious joy, feeling
reborn, releasing the past selves
The clock that yielding strikes twelve, a new
dawn, embracing awakening existence.
IV
Quasi-spurious enemy within, internal
scaramouch penumbra
Savvy Ex-Faustian machinations, baneful,
ever-screaming flame depleted.
New life evading the self-illusion, letting go
pernicious mesmerism
Empowered empyrean ambrosia, newly driven
toward vibrant polestar
In salient clement equanimity, finding a new
circumspect consciousness.

Astro-kittae

I am Astro Kitea, Also K177y, kitty, and BOSS.
I zoom the universe in my
Rocketship looking for big shiny rocks
I have a collection of red, green, and gold,
Purple, sage, vanilla, and blue
I even have one tiny rock
 that changes colors with my moods

I fly my ship through
The dark and past the shiny stars
I've been on visits to many worlds, even venus,
and mars
The moon was nice and the
Sun was so bright but
Earth is my favorite of them all.
We are all Earth cats of
Fame and fortune galore
Last month, O'Mally, a striped
Scottish fold caught us an invader,
A mouse by the name of Reginald
Who knew a mouse could cook
And he knows all the crew's favorite desserts.

There's a vision blue named natalia
With the best sense of direction
I've ever yet known

Dave the Siamese is good with computers
And on our weapons is Fitzgerald the
Old orange tabby whose moves are still ones to
behold.

Jenny Mainecoone is a master of science and
Skillful is mike with his catnip pipe
Giving advice and good feels.

Then there was Panaka, a Tonkinese ninja,
whose paws will heal anyone injured
Then there is me, a Devin Rex with a goatee,
and I am in charge of all of these.

Tomorrow I'll go far, when we cat friends
receive us a call.
But for now, I'll wait here, cuddled near you my
dear, purring with attention on pillow.

Umbrella Love

Where The Streets Have No Name.
I Played Chicken With The Train.
A Crazy Little Thing Called Love.

Let a Smile Be Your Umbrella.
For Your Love - Cinderella.
I Only Have Eyes for You.

Don't Let the Lights Go Out.
The Light Behind Your Eyes.
God Only Knows - I'll Catch You.

Something to be Proud Of.
The Only Exception.
My Girl - It Had to be You.

Umbrellas In The Rain.
Never Tear Us Apart.
Sea of Love - Eternal Flame.

Somewhere Over the Rainbow.
Rollercoaster of Love.
Vision of Love - Sarah Smiles.

Of Noble Birth

I was once a child of god
And then I came to earth
And while I may
Sometimes forget
I've always been of Noble Birth.

I am here, hear my prayers, return me safely
there.
To heaven's home, far above, in the sky
somewhere.
I know you're there in my hour of need.
To remind me who I am
To you I am and will always be
your child of special worth.

A child of God I remain.
Of this I have been taught.
But in this cold and fallen world,
That tries to bring me down,
Remembering is not so easy.

So I open my heart and try your words.
And in them my doubts are freed.
I struggle to know who I am.
So I let the spirit teach me.

I am here, hear my prayers, return me safely
there.
To heaven's home, far above, in the sky
somewhere.
I know you're there in my hour of need.
To remind me who I am
To you I am and will always be
your child of special worth.

In the struggle of self discovery
I feel the truth of me.
I am not lost or forgotten
By God or those who came before me.

They are here and will assist me
In my life long work.
With practice now I have learned
Skills and talents aplenty

And through this knowledge
And his love
I can bless the lives of many.
By patience and by practice
And an eye single to his glory.

I am here, hear my prayers, return me safely
there.

To heaven's home, far above, in the sky
somewhere.
I know you're there in my hour of need.
To remind me who I am
To you I am and will always be
your child of special worth.

I was once a child of god
And then I came to earth
And while I may
Sometimes forget
I've always been of Noble Birth.

A child of God I remain.
Here I stand in your care,
your love,
your truth.
And until that day we embrace again,
I'll embrace my spiritual worth.

CLAY IN TIME AND SPACE

TIME STANDS STILL
CLAY WITH HANDS SHIFTING
MUDD FROM THE SUN HOT
MOLDING ACROSS SPACE
SHAPE TAKEN FROM LIFE
SQUARE ROUND TRIANGULAR
BLUE RED AND GREEN
HUES COME TO LIFE
SOUGHT WITH TIME THROUGH
ETERNITY

KNOWLEDGE SHAPED SKILL
EMOTION FLUIDIC IN DRIFT
PEACE IN SOUND ALL AROUND
VENOM NOT EVER PRESENT
NO TIME FOR ANGER
NONE FOR REGRET OR GRIEF

THE CLAY SPINS FAST
IN POTTER'S HANDS
SHAPED WITH WIND AND HOPE
TOSSED AND BURNED BY THE SUN
TWISTED AND PULLED BY STRENGTH
THE TIME BEGINS TO MOVE

STRANGE AS FICTION, REAL AS LIFE
HARDENED BY FIRE HOT
WITH HEAT SEALED,
THE FIRE THEN TAMED ETERNAL

I AM HERE NOW CREATED
I AM FROM THE FIRE FORGED
I AM IN THIS LIFE PERFECTED
THROUGH TIME AND GRACE AND FORM
IN HIS HANDS I AM CHANGING
BECOMING SOMETHING NEW
AND IN ETERNAL PERSPECTIVE
WITH HIS HELP I'LL LIVE ONCE MORE

LOVE (My First Poem)

Hate is weaker than love. Love will always triumph. Hate will always lose. Love comes from the heart, hate comes from the mind. What comes from the heart is pure, what comes from the mind is often unfair and hateful. Life is precious. Life is pure. Love is pure. Hate is bad and evil. Love is life. Life is love. Hearts are always pure but the mind can corrupt the heart. True love is pure like the dove, pure and true. Truth will always prevail at the end of mortal life. Life lives forever and never ends.

Some say life is like a predator stalking it's prey. But life is like a friend with us on the journey. Temples are forever, including our bodies. They are like temples that can grow stronger or be torn down by hate and evil. However, if you take care of your temple you will have joy.

Blessings last forever with God and you together. Love can be a blessing or like a sharp needle poking you in the side. Love is not always true but can be as true as the sun will rise.

Vengeance is evil, so is fear. They can only conquer those who let them. Hate can be strong or you can have no hate at all, depending on what you feel.

Feelings can be strong or weak. Love can be like God's love, unbreakable, impenetrable, kind but stern. We must all help each other to grow stronger.

Helping others and yourself to grow stronger in mental and spiritual strength makes you both feel good. Being kind to others is being more like Christ and God. GREAT BLESSINGS COME TO THOSE WHO IT, NEED IT AND HELP THEMSELVES TO GET IT. Being boss and being bossy are two different things. Being boss is having control, being bossy is misusing that control. Control is good if used right.

Love is a higher feeling. So is kindness and meekness. Fear and hate are lowest. Happiness is truer than hate.

Life is like a landscape, always changing, always evolving. Life is like a book. You never know what will happen in the next chapter. Life is like a play put on by God, with us being the characters.

Life can be as mean as a monster or as calm as a lamb. Life can roar like a tiger or meow like a housecat. Life can be as fast as a cheetah or as slow as a turtle.

We are all on a journey, with God lighting the way back to Him. Life is like a circus with God training us to obey His commandments. The Calliope music in the sound from the heart.

Christ my Savior King of Love

Christ my Savior, my God and King, for him I have surely seen. And many will say that what I write here this day can only be but a fable.

To them I would say have faith on me this day as I share with you something quite personal.

There was once a time before rhythm and rhyme when I was rambunctious, rowdy, and rude, ADD bouncy with autistic understanding and Tourette's wrapped up in an Ivan suit.

This is when I begin on a night like many others. With frustration and anger and NO's, A fight was underway with my mother that day and stress without mercy arose.

I don't remember why, but tempers were sky high, and to my room I was told I must go. And to my room there I went with tears where I was sent with fear in my heart I did go.

I remember the feeling of being a burden and trying to understand what I had done wrong.

For you must see that for someone like me
understanding can be a great burden. When we
get things right to us it is a delight but often it
seems many mistakes do we need, before right
we do make on our tries.

I could not understand why what I'd done was
deemed 'bad' and was called stupid and then
sent away

To my room I did fly, and in my corner I did cry
as I wished for existence to be over. And there I
did stay alone on that day till something quite
brilliant did happen.

It was not dark but the lights they were off as I
sat on my bed in the basement. Yet to my
surprise it suddenly became bright and there was
someone beside me.

I can't fully describe what happened that day, for
much that was said, while still in my head, has
been blocked from my still active memory

This I can say—that He did appear to me that day,
at the tender young age of seven.

While some may not believe that this happened
to me, in scripture we find examples. Did Christ
not say to his apostles "suffer the children, and
forbid them not to come unto me."

Herein is what I was allowed to remember. For I
now understand that with this God among men, I
heard things not yet able to be uttered.

Next to me he did sit and spoke to me calmly
and for me I was never afraid. For I knew him as
surely as I now know my right hand.

He was a dear friend, and a deeper connection
with someone I have never since felt. Even with
my wife I love dearly, I have never felt so
clearly, as I did on that day at age seven.

And within this safety he taught me exactly what
it was that I had done wrong. In that moment
was a gift I've rarely experienced since–a
moment of perfect clarity.

It seems we spoke without speaking and pure
thought was sent and received. Then we played a
game with my toys before it was time for him to
leave.

Some may say it was an angel I saw that day.
But I know what I saw is true. And even though
my memory is blocked from seeing his hands or
his feet, of him I am sure I knew. For I said this
to my mom while in white, not red, he otherwise
looked like Del Parson's painting 'Jesus the
Christ' on my wall.

www.ingramcontent.com/pod-product-compliance
Lightning Source LLC
LaVergne TN
LVHW010915200726
843509LV00013B/1952